About the Author

Mr. Sagar Salunke has 10 years of experience in automation testing including QTP(UFT) and Selenium Webdriver in Java and C#. He has worked on large investment banking projects in tier-1 Software Companies in India, USA, UK, Australia and Switzerland.

He has designed automation frameworks in QTP that is widely used in the IT industry.

His hobbies include travelling to new tourist places, watching basketball, cricket and learning latest technological stuff.

A special note of Thanks to My Wife

I would like to dedicate this book to my lovely wife Priyanka for loving me so much and helping me write this book. Without her support, this book would not have been a reality.

Preface

QTP is the most popular automation tool in the market. It supports wide variety of applications in environments like .Net, Java, Web, Peoplesoft etc

In this book I have included all concepts related to QTP and vbscript with examples.

For latest updates on QTP, you can visit my blog at below url.

http://www.qtp-interview-questions.blogspot.com

Table of Contents

1. QTP Basic Concepts

1.1 Why Automation Testing

Software testing is the process to check if product complies with the user requirements. Now to test any software application, we can execute the test cases to validate each requirement of the product. We can test the product either manually or automatically.

In manual testing, testers verify and validate the application requirements manually. But in automation testing is done automatically by the automation tool like QTP or Selenium or Rational Robot.

I have listed some of the advantages of automation testing.

1. Faster Test Execution
2. Effort Saving
3. Time Saving
4. Accurate Testing

1.2 Why QTP?

Currently QTP is widely used in the automation industry due to it's ease of use and the number of environments it supports. QTP can be used to test applications based upon various technologies like .NET, Web Based, Java based etc.

You can install QTP – demo version by downloading it from hp website.

1.3 Record and Playback in QTP

Writing a script in QTP is very simple. You can just record an application and script is automatically created.

When you open QTP, you can see one button called record. You can click on it to start recording. You can use the sample flight application for recording purpose.

After I recorded the sample flight application, below code was automatically created.

```
Dialog("Login").Activate

Dialog("Login").WinEdit("Agent Name:").Set "sagar"

Dialog("Login").WinEdit("Agent Name:").Type  micTab

Dialog("Login").WinEdit("Password:").SetSecure
"52ff9c3a11cd29043aa16192c652a6303bcda44d"

Dialog("Login").WinButton("OK").Click

Dialog("Login").Dialog("Flight
Reservations").WinButton("OK").Click
```

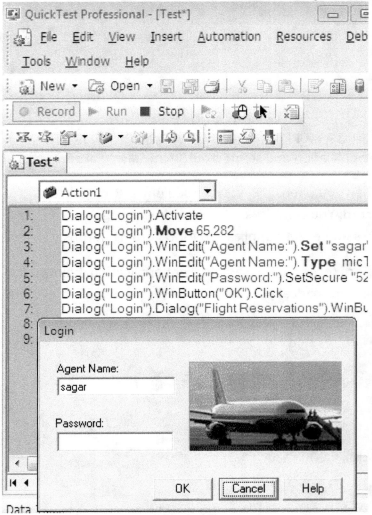

Figure 1 - Record and Playback in QTP

Let me explain you the above code. In line no 1, Dialog is the name of class. Login is the name of object of type Dialog. And Activate is a method of the class Dialog. So basic syntax is same for all lines. That means you have to specify the name of class and then name of the object.

After you get reference to the object, you can explore the properties and methods of that object. QTP provides one tool called object spy (discussed below) which can be used to get the details about properties and methods of the object.

1.4 Object Spy in QTP

As seen in below figure, we can use object spy in QTP to learn the properties and methods of the objects in the application.

Object spy helps us find

1. Test object properties and methods
2. Run time object properties and methods

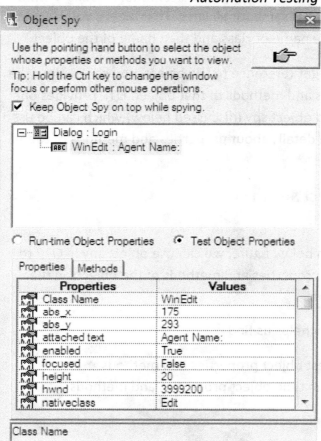

Figure 2 - Object Spy in QTP

1.5 Object Repository in QTP

Object repository is another important concept in QTP. When we record the application in QTP, the objects are stored in the repository called object repository.

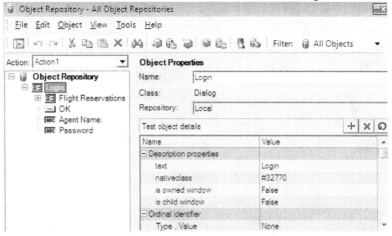

Figure 3 - Local Object Repository in QTP

There are 2 kinds of object repositories in QTP.

1. Local
2. Shared

By default objects are stored in local object repository .
We can follow the steps given below to create a shared
Object Repository in QTP.

1. Open Local Or
2. Go to File->Export Local Objects
3. Save file as abc.tsr

So abc.tsr will be a shared OR and we can associate it with
any test.

Difference between local and shared OR is given below

1. Local OR is used by only one action in Test While Shared OR can be used by multiple actions and tests
2. Local OR can be edited without OR manager While shared OR can be edited by using only OR manager
3. We cannot merge 2 local OR but we can merge 2 shared ORs using OR manager
4. We cannot compare 2 local OR but we can compare 2 shared ORs using OR manager
5. We can associate/disassociate the shared OR to test at run time but Local OR is associated to test at any time by default.
6. Extension of the shared OR is .tsr while Local OR is .mtr
7. When we export the Local OR, shared OR is created.

Object repository manager in QTP.

Object repository manager in QTP is very important tool to manage the shared object repository. Please note that you can't use Object repository manager in QTP to manage local object repository.

Below are the main uses of Object repository manager in QTP.

1. Open and edit shared object repository (TSR files).
2. Compare 2 shared Object repositories in QTP.
3. Merge 2 shared Object repositories in QTP.

we can associate object repository to QTP Test either manually or by automation code.

Manually with Test Settings - In this method you have to go to Resources->Associate repositories. Here you can give the path of tsr file that is Shared OR.

By Automation Code, You have to use repositories collection object as mentioned in below code.

```
Dim QTPAPP
Dim qtObjRes
Set QTPAPP= CreateObject("QuickTest.Application")
QTPAPP.Launch
QTPAPP.Visible = True
QTPAPP.Open "C:\Test\Testabc", False, False
Set qtObjRes = QTPAPP.Test.Actions ("Login").ObjectRepositories
qtObjRes.Add "C:\OR\myRes.tsr", 1
```

1.6 Object Identification Mechanism in QTP

It is very important to understand the object identification mechanism in QTP.

Object identification in QTP is based on 4 types of properties and an ordinal identifier.

1. Mandatory properties
2. Assistive properties
3. Base Filter properties
4. Optional Filter properties

We can specify the list of mandatory properties, assistive properties, base filter properties, optional filter properties and ordinal identifier.

While recording the application, qtp will use mandatory properties to identify the object. If all mandatory properties are not sufficient then assistive properties are used for identifying the object uniquely.

If assistive properties are not sufficient to identify the object uniquely then ordinal identifier is used to identify the object.

Now let us try to understand the ordinal identifiers in QTP.

There are 3 types of ordinal identifiers.

1. **Location** – based upon the position of object
2. **Index** – based upon index of object
3. **Creation Time** – based upon time at which object is created. (Browser object)

1.7 Checkpoints in QTP

Checkpoints are used to verify the property values with expected ones. If they match checkpoints pass else they fail. You can add standard checkpoint by right clicking the statement and then selecting the insert standard checkpoint menu.

Sample checkpoint window is shown in below fig.

Browser("Google").Page("Google").WebEdit("q").Set "salunke"
Browser("Google").Page("Google").WebEdit("q").Check
CheckPoint("q_2")
Browser("Google").Page("Google").WebEdit("q").Output
CheckPoint("q")
Browser("Google").Page("Google").WebButton("Google Search").Click

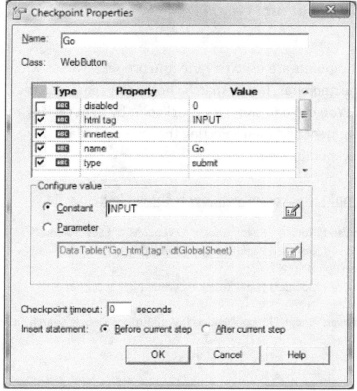

Figure 4 - Inserting Standard Checkpoint

You can insert the following checkpoint types to check various objects in an application.

Standard Checkpoint checks the property value of an object in your application. The standard checkpoint checks a variety of objects such as buttons, radio buttons, combo boxes, lists, and so forth. For example, you can check that a radio button is activated after it is selected or you can check the value of an edit box.

Image Checkpoint checks the value of an image in your application. For example, you can check that a selected image's source file is correct.

Bitmap Checkpoint checks an area of your application as a bitmap. For example, suppose you have a Web site that can display a map of a city the user specifies. The map has control keys for zooming. You can record the new map that is displayed after one click on the control key that zooms in the map. Using the bitmap checkpoint, you can check that the map zooms in correctly.

Table Checkpoint checks information within a table. For example, suppose your application contains a table listing all available flights from New York to San Francisco. You can add a table checkpoint to check that the time of the first flight in the table is correct.

Text Checkpoint checks that a text string is displayed in the appropriate place on a Web page or application. For example, suppose a Web page displays the sentence Flight departing from New York to San Francisco. You can create a text checkpoint that checks that the words "New York" are displayed between "Flight departing from" and "to San Francisco".

Text Area Checkpoint checks that a text string is displayed within a defined area in a Windows-based application, according to specified criteria. For example, suppose your Visual Basic application has a button that says View Doc <Num>, where <Num> is replaced by the four digit code entered in a form elsewhere in the application. You can create a text area checkpoint to confirm that the number displayed on the button is the same as the number entered in the form.

Accessibility Checkpoint identifies areas of your Web site that may not conform to the World Wide Web Consortium (W3C) Web Content Accessibility Guidelines. For example, guideline 1.1 of the W3C Web Content Accessibility Guidelines requires you to provide a text equivalent for every non-text element. You can add an Alt property check to check whether objects that require the Alt property under this guideline, do in fact have this tag.

Page Checkpoint checks the characteristics of a Web page. For example, you can check how long a Web page takes to load or whether a Web page contains broken links.

Database Checkpoint checks the contents of a database accessed by your application. For example, you can use a database checkpoint to check the contents of a database containing flight information for your Web site.

XML Checkpoint checks the data content of XML documents in XML files or XML documents in Web pages and frames.

1.8 Reporter Object

The object used for sending information to the test results.

Reporter.ReportEvent EventStatus, ReportStepName, Details [, ImageFilePath]

EventStatus Number or pre-defined constant Status of the Test Results step:

1. 0 or micPass
2. 1 or micFail
3. 2 or micDone
4. 3 or micWarning

Reporter.Filter

Filter property is used to filter the results based on below values

1. 0 or rfEnableAll Default. All reported events are displayed in the Test Results.
2. 1 or rfEnableErrorsAndWarnings only event with a warning or fail status are displayed in the Test Results.
3. 2 or rfEnableErrorsOnly Only events with a fail status are displayed in the Test Results.
4. 3 or rfDisableAll No events are displayed in the Test Results.

Reporter. ReportPath

The following example uses the ReportPath property to retrieve the folder in which the results are stored and displays the folder in a message box.

```
Dim Path
Path = Reporter.ReportPath
'path where results are stored
Print path
```

Reporter. RunStatus

The following example uses the RunStatus property to retrieve the status of the run session at a specific point.

Print Reporter.RunStatus

1.9 Test Settings in QTP

Test settings is very important part of the QTP test. You can open the test settings from the file sub menu.

You will find below sections in test settings window.

1. Properties Settings:

In properties section you will find the location of the test and add-ins associated with the test.

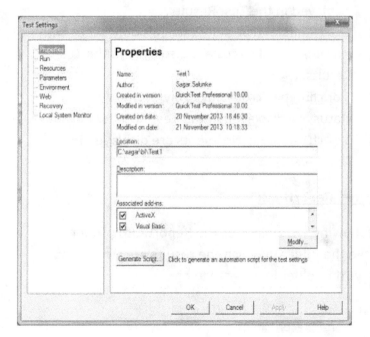

2. Run Settings:

In run section you will find below settings.

Data table iterations

When error occurs - what to do

Object Synchronization timeout

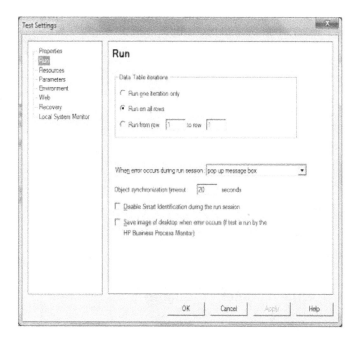

3. Resources Settings:

In resources section you will be able to see/edit the associated function libraries of the test.

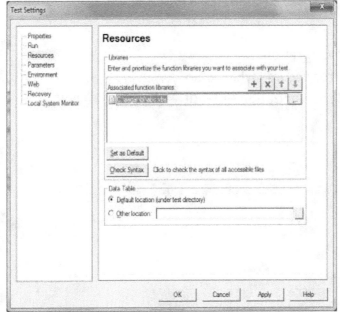

4. Parameters Settings:

In parameters section you will specify the input and ouptu parameters.

You can access the parameters using script as mentioned below.

Set qtApp = CreateObject("QuickTest.Application") ' Create the Application object
Set pDefColl = qtApp.Test.ParameterDefinitions
Set rtParams = pDefColl.GetParameters() ' Retrieve the Parameters collection defined for the test.
Set rtParam = rtParams.Item("sagar") ' Retrieve a specific

21

parameter.

print rtParam.value

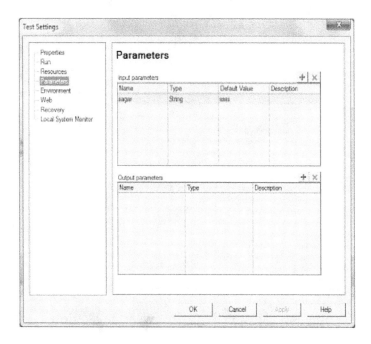

5. Environment Settings:

In Environment section you can view built - in and user defined global variables. You can also create new user defined variables here.

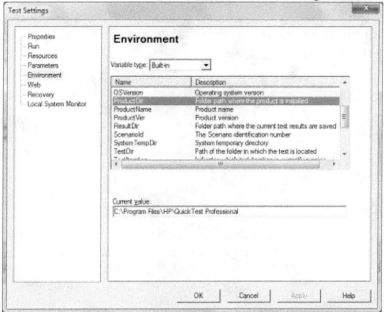

6. Web Settings:

In web section you can specify the browser navigation timeout.

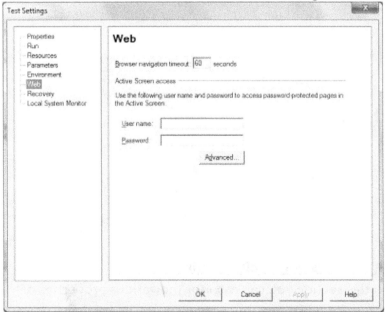

7. Recovery Settings:

In recovery section you will be able to add and activate/deactivate new recovery scenarios to the test. You can also view the properties of the scenarios.

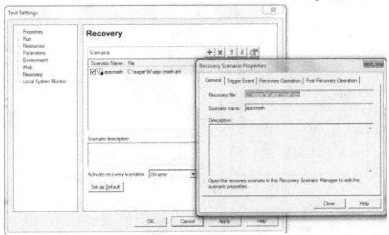

8. Local System Monitor Settings:

In this section you can monitor the various properties of the system like memory usage, cpu usage by given application during test execution.

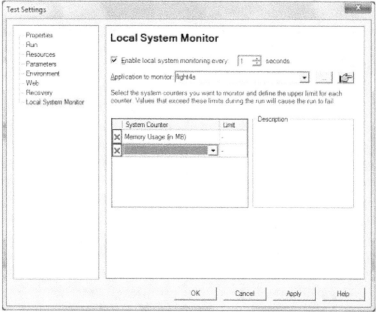

1.10 MercuryTimers in QTP

MercuryTimers can be used to measure the passage of time in milliseconds.

retTime = MercuryTimers.Timer(TimerName).ElapsedTime

Returns the total accumulated time in milliseconds since the timer started. The ElapsedTime property is the default property for the MercuryTimer object.

```
MercuryTimers("Timer1").Start
'Start measuring time using Timer1.
Wait 1
MercuryTimers("Timer1").Stop
```

26

'After one second, stop Timer1.
'Two seconds later, restart Timer1 (which will continue to measure time from 'the time it stopped).
Wait 2
MercuryTimers("Timer1").Continue

2. QTP Advanced Concepts

2.1 Descriptive Programming

Descriptive programming is used to identify objects that are created at runtime and we can't really store them in Object Repository.

There are 2 types of description programming.
1. Static Descriptive programming
2. Dynamic Descriptive programming

Static Descriptive programming Example -

```
Browser("index:=0").page("title:=Google").webedit("name:=q").set
"xyz"
```

Dynamic Descriptive programming Example -
```
'Find all edit boxes on google page using descriptive programming
Set descriptionObject = Description.Create()
descriptionObject("micclass").value = "webedit"
descriptionObject("outerhtml").value = ".*input.*"
descriptionObject("outerhtml").regularexpression = true

set col =
Browser("index:=0").page("title:=Google").childobjects(descriptionObj
ect)
print "Total edit boxes on the page" & col.count
For i=0 to col.count-1
 print col(i).getROProperty("outerhtml")
Next
```

Regular Expressions in Static descriptive programming in QTP.

Browser("index:=0").page("title:=Google").Webedit("name
:=q").set "sagar salunke"
Browser("creationtime:=0").page("title:=Google").Webbut
ton("name:=Google.*").Click

Please note that last statement uses regular expression to identify the button whose name starts with Google.
If your property value itself contains the special character then that should be escaped using \ character.

Example - Suppose you want to click on the link "+sagar". Now this link contains the special character +. To click on this link, we can use below code
Browser("creationtime:=0").page("title:=Google").Link("in
nertext:=\+sagar").Click

Regular Expressions in Dynamic descriptive programming in QTP.

Set descriptionObject = Description.Create()
descriptionObject("innertext").value = "+sagar"
descriptionObject("innertext").RegularExpression = false

'Please note that we can specify whether the value is regular expression or not using RegularExpression property. By default it is true.

Browser("index:=0").page("title:=Google").Link(description Object).click

This is how we can use Regular Expressions in QTP

<u>When should we use Descriptive Programming</u>

1. When you are creating functions in an external file which is used by multiple actions.
2. The objects in the application are dynamic in nature like many similar links...
3. When object repository is getting huge due to the no. of objects being added.

2.2 Recovery Scenarios in QTP

Recovery scenarios are used to handle the unexpected events in QTP.

Using **recovery scenario manager** you can create new recovery scenarios and store it in a file with .qrs extension. One qrs file may contain multiple recovery scenarios.

To create new recovery scenario, click on the button circled with red color. It will open recovery scenario wizard.

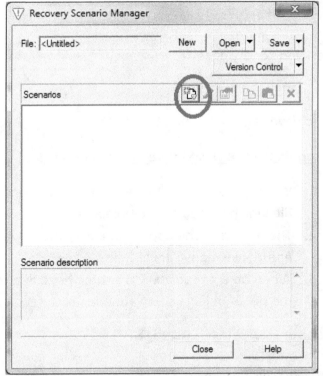

Open Recovery Scenario Wizard.Recovery scenario wizard
shows the steps involved in creating the recovery scenario.
Click on Next

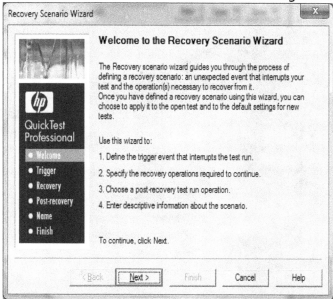

Select Trigger Event.There are 4 types of the trigger events.

1. Pop up window
2. Object State
3. Test Run Error
4. Application Crash

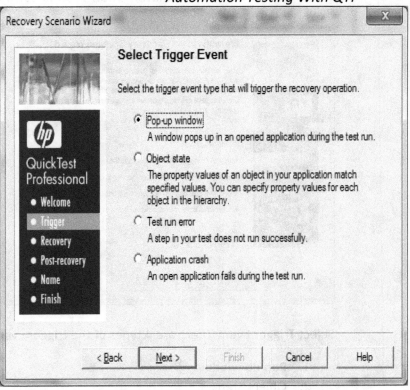

Specify the trigger Details. In this step you have to specify more details about the trigger. For example if you selected pop up window in trigger event above, you will have to provide the title or text of the pop up as shown below.

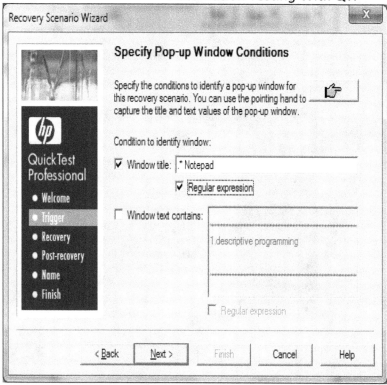

Recovery Operation. After specifying the trigger event, you have to provide the recovery operation. There are 4 types of the recovery operations.

1. Keyboard or mouse operation
2. Close application process
3. Function Call
4. Restart Microsoft Windows

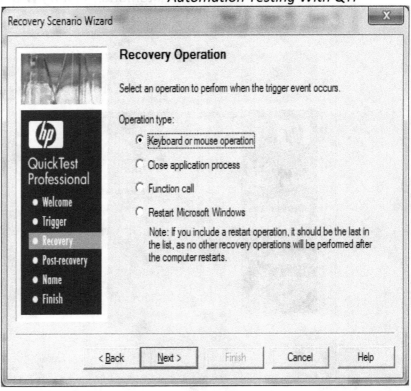

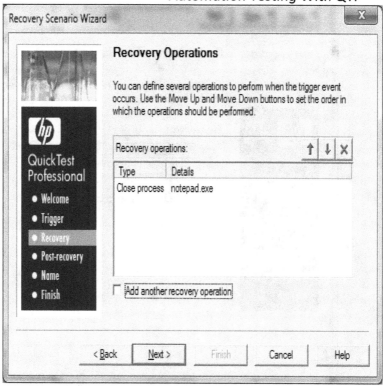

Post Recovery Operation.

In Post Recovery You can tell what step should be executed after recovery is done by QTP.

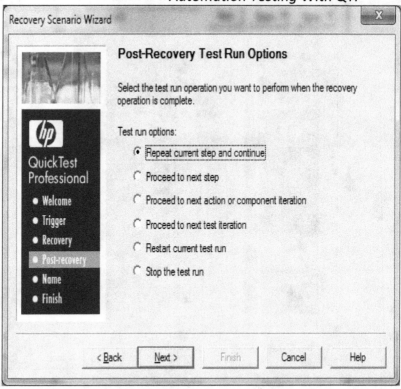

Name the Recovery Scenario.

You have to give the name to recovery scenario in this step

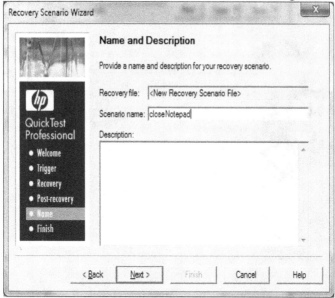

Finishing the recovery scenario.

This is last step. You can add this scenario to current test in this step.

Once you click finish recovery scenario manager window will be shown where you can save the qrs file.

Please note that to activate recovery scenario, you have to go to test settings.

Recovery scenarios are saved in recovery scenario files having the extension .qrs. A recovery scenario file is a logical collection of recovery scenarios, grouped according to your own specific requirements.

Recovery object can be used to handle the recovery scenarios programmatically.

	Activate
Recovery Methods	GetScenarioName
	GetScenarioPosition

	GetScenarioStatus
	SetScenarioStatus
Recovery Properties	Count Property
	Enabled Property

```
msgbox Recovery.Count        // Number of Recovery Scenarios
msgbox Recovery              //Is Recovery enabled?"
For Iter = 1 to Recovery.Count
    Recovery.GetScenarioName Iter, ScenarioFile, ScenarioName
    Position = Recovery.GetScenarioPosition( ScenarioFile,
ScenarioName )
    msgbox Recovery.GetScenarioStatus( Position ),, "Is scenario " &_
    ScenarioName & " from " & ScenarioFile & " enabled ?"
Next
```

2.3 RepositoriesCollection Object in QTP

You can manage the shared object repositories using RepositoriesCollection object. It contains the same set of object repository files as the Associated Repository Files tab of the Action Properties dialog box. The operations you perform on the RepositoriesCollection object affect only the run-time copy of the collection.

You use the RepositoriesCollection object to associate or disassociate shared object repositories with an action during a run session.

For example, suppose you want to test a Web application that supports twenty different languages. Instead of creating twenty different tests (one for each supported language), you can create one test and run multiple iterations of that test—one for each language version of your application. If you create one or more shared object repository files for each version, you can use the RepositoriesCollection object to load the required shared object repository files for each iteration. Then, when each iteration finishes, you can use the RepositoriesCollection object to remove these object repository files prior to loading the object repository files required for the next iteration.

RepositoriesCollection Methods	Add
	Find
	MoveToPos
	Remove
	RemoveAll
RepositoriesCollection Properties	Count
	Item

Below example illustrates how we can use this object in qtp.

```
Dim QTPAPP
Dim qtObjRes
Set QTPAPP= CreateObject("QuickTest.Application")
QTPAPP.Launch
```

QTPAPP.Visible = True
QTPAPP.Open "C:\Test\Testabc", False, False
Set qtObjRes = QTPAPP.Test.Actions ("Login").ObjectRepositories
qtObjRes.Add "C:\OR\myRes.tsr", 1

2.4 DotNetFactory in QTP

In QTP, you can use dotnetfactory object to access .net objects. You must have .net framework installed in your system before you use createinstance method.

It enables you to create an instance of a .NET object, and access its methods and properties. Createinstance method returns a COM interface for a .NET object.

Syntax

Set myobj = DotNetFactory.CreateInstance (TypeName [,Assembly] [,args])

Here

Typename - any type name that .net framework provides

Examples using dotnetfactory

The following example uses the CreateInstance method to create a object of a system environment type

```
Set obj = Dotnetfactory.CreateInstance("System.Environment")
print obj.MachineName
```

The following example uses the CreateInstance method to create a object of a DateTime type

```
Set DateTime = Dotnetfactory.CreateInstance("System.DateTime")
Set oDate = DateTime.Parse("9 Jan 1986")
DesiredDateFormat = oDate.Day & "/" & oDate.Month & "/" &
oDate.Year
msgbox DesiredDateFormat
```

Thus we can easily change the date format in QTP using dotnetfactory object in QTP.

Another example to show the windows form in QTP.

Below script will show windows form with text as - Total number of test cases executed

```
Set MyMsgBox =
DotNetFactory.CreateInstance("System.Windows.Forms.Form","Syste
m.Windows.Forms")

MyForm.Text = "Total number of test cases executed "

MyForm.show()
```

2.5 Datatables in QTP

Datatable is just like a excel workbook. In datatable we can have many sheets.
When we design a test automation framework in qtp, we usually store the test data inside excel sheets.

Sometimes we need to load the test data in datatable to execute the test cases.

We can either import all excel sheets from excel workbook or we can import particular excel sheet from the the workbook to the datatable

To import all sheets from excel file, use below line of code
datatable.Import "c:\abc.xls"

To import single sheet from excel file, use below line of code
'here we are importing the sheet global from abc.xls into testdata sheet in Data table in QTP.

datatable.AddSheet "testdata"
datatable.ImportSheet "c:\abc.xls","Global","testdata"

2.6 Quality Center and QTP integration

We can connect to quality center easily using the below window. You can open below window from the file menu of QTP.

You have to provide the address of server and click on connect. Once server is found, you will be asked for the QC credentials and project to connect to and then you can view test plan in the QC.

Before you work with QC-QTP integration, ensure that you have set up below things.

1. Install QC add-in for QTP
2. Install QTP add-in for QC

You should also ensure that you have selected below checkbox in options window.

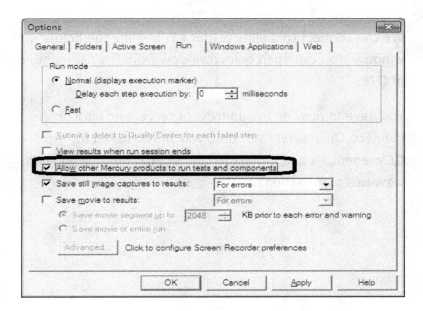

2.7 Crypt Object in QTP

Crypt object is used to encrypt the confidential data like passwords in QTP.

You can use setSecure method to set the encrypted data in the edit box like password. This will ensure that no one will be able to view your actual password.

QTP also provides password encoder tool to convert the plain texts into encoded strings as displayed below.

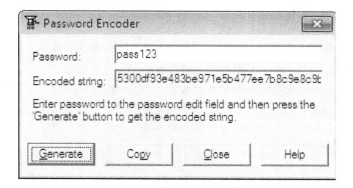

Figure 5 - Password Encoder

2.8 Environment Object in QTP

Environment object is used work with global variables.

In QTP, there are mainly 2 types of environment variables.

1. Built In
2. User Defined

Built in environment variables are read only. for example

```
print environment("LocalHostName")
' print machine name
```

User defined environment variables can be modified.

There are 2 types of user defined environment variables in QTP.

1. Internal - can be modified. They are defined in test settings.
2. External - read only . They are loaded from external file.

We can create environment variables at runtime using below code. In below example we have created an environment variable called MyDirectory and stored a value – "c:\test"

```
Environment.Value("MyDirectory") = "c:\test"
```

We can load the values from the external file as well using below syntax.

```
Environment.LoadFromFile "c:\Env.ini"
' Load varaibles from ENV.ini
```

Format of ini file should be like this -

```
[Environment]
  var1=abcd
  var2=xyz
[Environment]
```

2.9 Scheduling QTP scripts

We can schedule the qtp scripts to run at specific time using windows scheduler. We can create a vbs file with below code to execute qtp script as a job.

```
'Create the instance of qtp application
Set qtApp = CreateObject("QuickTest.Application")

'launch qtp
qtApp.Launch

'Make the qtp window visible
qtApp.Visible = True

'open the test you want to open
qtApp.Open "F:\qtp\dotnetfactory", True

' Run the test
qtApp.Test.Run

' Close the test
qtApp.Test.Close

'close the application
qtApp.quit
```

2.10 Automation Frameworks in QTP

Automation framework is designed to ease the process of test automation using QTP. Automation framework helps from scalability point of view. It is very easy to automate the test cases using automation framework rather than ad hoc approach.

There are mainly 3 types of Automation Frameworks in QTP

1. Keyword Driven Framework

2. Data Driven Framework

3. Hybrid Framework

Keyword Driven Framework :
In Keyword Driven Framework , Importance is given to functions than Test Data. when we have to test multiple functionality we can go for keyword frameworks. Each keyword is mapped to function in QTP library and application.

DATA Driven Framework :
In data driven framework, importance is given to test data than multiple functionality of application. We design data driven framework to work with applications where we want to test same flow with different test data.

Hybrid Framework -
This is the combination of keyword and data driven frameworks.

After analyzing the application, you can decide what kind of framework best suits your needs and then you can design automation framework in QTP.

Keyword driven automation framework in QTP

Keyword driven Automation Framework is most popular QTP framework. It is very easy to design and learn a keyword driven automation framework in QTP.

In this article I will explain you all details about how we can design and use keyword driven automation framework in QTP with example. I will also explain the advantages and disadvantages of keyword driven automation framework in QTP.

In keyword driven automation framework, focus is mainly on kewords/functions and not the test data. This means we focus on creating the functions that are mapped to the functionality of the application.

For example - Suppose you have a flight reservation application which provides many features like

1. Login to the application
2. Search Flights
3. Book Flight tickets
4. Cancel Tickets
5. Fax Order
6. View Reports

To implement the keyword driven automation framework for this kind of application we will create functions in vbscript for each functionality mentioned above. We pass the test data and test object details to these functions.

50

The main components of keyword driven automation framework in QTP

Each keyword driven automation framework has some common components as mentioned below.

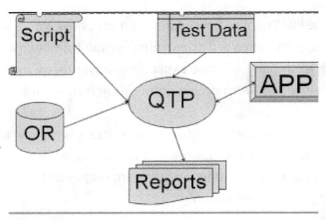

As dispalyed in above image, We have 5 main components in **keyword driven automation framework**

    1. Scripts Library (.vbs, .txt, .qfl)
    2. OR - Object Repository
    3. Test Data (generally in excel format)
    4. QTP - Settings and Environment Variables
    5. Reports - (Generally in HTML format)
    6. Test Driver Script/ Test Engine

Generally automated test cases are stored in excel sheets. From QTP ,we read excel file and then row by row we execute the functions in a test case. Each test case is implemented as a set of keywords.

Common columns in Data sheet are mentioned below.

1. Test case ID - Stores the Test Case ID mapped to Manual Test Cases.
2. Test Case Name - Name of the Test cases/ Scenario.
3. Execute Flag - if Marked Y -> Test case will be executed
4. Test_Step_Id - Steps in a test case
5. Keyword - Mapped to function in library file.
6. Object Types - Class of the object e.g winedit, webedit, swfbutton etc
7. Object Names -Names of objects in OR .
8. Object Values - Actual test data to be entered in the objects.
9. Parameter1 - This is used to control the execution flow in the function.

Test_ID	TC_Name	Execute	Test_Step_ID	Keyword	Object_Types	Object_Names	Object_Values	Parameter1
1	Login To App	Y	Step1	login	winedit,winedit	userid,password	salunke,mercury	
			Step2	Insert_Order	wincombobox,wincombobo	flyfrom,flyto	london,paris	
			Step3	Fax_Order				Order_Id

Please note that this is just a sample data sheet that can be used in keyword driven framework. There could be customized data sheets for each project depending upon the requirement and design.

For example there could be more parameters or test data is stored in the databases.

Driver script is the main script that interacts with all modules mentioned above.

Main tasks that are accomplished by driver script are ->

1. Read data from the **Environment variables** /File or from **ini file.**
2. Call report module to create Report folders / files
3. **Import Excel sheet to Data table.**
4. **Read Excel file.**
5. Call the function mapped to keyword.
6. Log the result

3. Working with Databases in QTP

3.1 Database Access using vbscript

```
Set conn = CreateObject("ADODB.Connection")
conn.Provider="Microsoft.Jet.OLEDB.4.0"
conn.Open("dsn=abc")
set rs = CreateObject("ADODB.recordset")
rs.Open "Select * from Customers", conn

do until rs.EOF
   for each x in rs.Fields
       Response.Write(x.name)
       Response.Write(x.value & "<br />")
   next
rs.MoveNext

loop

rs.close
conn.close
```

3.2 SQL Queries

SQL Statement	Syntax
AND / OR	SELECT column_name(s) FROM table_name WHERE condition

	AND|OR condition
ALTER TABLE	ALTER TABLE table_name ADD column_name datatype or ALTER TABLE table_name DROP COLUMN column_name
AS (alias)	SELECT column_name AS column_alias FROM table_name or SELECT column_name FROM table_name AS table_alias
BETWEEN	SELECT column_name(s) FROM table_name WHERE column_name BETWEEN value1 AND value2
CREATE DATABASE	CREATE DATABASE database_name
CREATE TABLE	CREATE TABLE table_name (column_name1 data_type, column_name2 data_type, column_name2 data_type, ...

	)
CREATE INDEX	CREATE INDEX index_name ON table_name (column_name) or CREATE UNIQUE INDEX index_name ON table_name (column_name)
CREATE VIEW	CREATE VIEW view_name AS SELECT column_name(s) FROM table_name WHERE condition ---Views are used for security, simplicity. ---Materialised view is used in datawarehousing and it contains replica of database
DELETE	DELETE FROM table_name WHERE some_column=some_value or DELETE FROM table_name (Note: Deletes the entire table!!) DELETE * FROM table_name (Note: Deletes the entire table!!)

DROP DATABASE	DROP DATABASE database_name
DROP INDEX	DROP INDEX table_name.index_name (SQL Server) DROP INDEX index_name ON table_name (MS Access) DROP INDEX index_name (DB2/Oracle) ALTER TABLE table_name DROP INDEX index_name (MySQL)
DROP TABLE	DROP TABLE table_name
GROUP BY	SELECT column_name, aggregate_function(column_name) FROM table_name WHERE column_name operator value GROUP BY column_name
HAVING	SELECT column_name, aggregate_function(column_name) FROM table_name WHERE column_name operator value GROUP BY column_name HAVING aggregate_function(column_name) operator value
IN	SELECT column_name(s) FROM table_name WHERE column_name

	IN (value1,value2,..)
INSERT INTO	INSERT INTO table_name VALUES (value1, value2, value3,....) *or* INSERT INTO table_name (column1, column2, column3,...) VALUES (value1, value2, value3,....)
INNER JOIN	SELECT column_name(s) FROM table_name1 INNER JOIN table_name2 ON table_name1.column_name=table_name2.col umn_name
LEFT JOIN	SELECT column_name(s) FROM table_name1 LEFT JOIN table_name2 ON table_name1.column_name=table_name2.col umn_name
RIGHT JOIN	SELECT column_name(s) FROM table_name1 RIGHT JOIN table_name2 ON table_name1.column_name=table_name2.col umn_name

FULL JOIN	SELECT column_name(s) FROM table_name1 FULL JOIN table_name2 ON table_name1.column_name=table_name2.column_name
LIKE	SELECT column_name(s) FROM table_name WHERE column_name LIKE pattern
ORDER BY	SELECT column_name(s) FROM table_name ORDER BY column_name [ASC|DESC]
SELECT DISTINCT	SELECT DISTINCT column_name(s) FROM table_name
SELECT INTO	SELECT * INTO new_table_name [IN externaldatabase] FROM old_table_name SELECT column_name(s) INTO new_table_name [IN externaldatabase] FROM old_table_name
SELECT TOP	SELECT TOP number|percent column_name(s) FROM table_name

TRUNCATE TABLE	TRUNCATE TABLE table_name
	Difference between truncate and drop :-
	Drop will destroy table completely.
	Truncate will destroy only records..Autocommited and fast
UNION	SELECT column_name(s) FROM table_name1 UNION SELECT column_name(s) FROM table_name2
UNION ALL	SELECT column_name(s) FROM table_name1 UNION ALL SELECT column_name(s) FROM table_name2
UPDATE	UPDATE table_name SET column1=value, column2=value,... WHERE some_column=some_value
WHERE	SELECT column_name(s) FROM table_name WHERE column_name operator value

3.3 SQL Aggregate Functions

SQL aggregate functions return a single value, calculated from values in a column.

AVG() - Returns the average value

COUNT() - Returns the number of rows

FIRST() - Returns the first value

LAST() - Returns the last value

MAX() - Returns the largest value

MIN() - Returns the smallest value

SUM() - Returns the sum

3.4 SQL Scalar functions

SQL scalar functions return a single value, based on the input value.

UCASE() - Converts a field to upper case

LCASE() - Converts a field to lower case

MID() - Extract characters from a text field

LEN() - Returns the length of a text field

ROUND() - Rounds a numeric field to the number of decimals specified

NOW() - Returns the current system date and time

4. VB Script

Vbscript is used as a scripting language in QTP. So understanding vbscript is a key to success in QTP. We will see important topics in vbscript in below sections.

4.1 Variables and data types in Vbscript

All variables in vbscript have default data type called variant. The data type of the variables changes as per the value stored in the variable.

We can have below sub-data types in the vbscript.

Subtype	Description
Empty	Variant is uninitialized. Value is 0 for numeric variables or a zero-length string ("") for string variables.
Null	Variant intentionally contains no valid data.
Boolean	Contains either <u>True</u> or <u>False</u>.
Byte	Contains integer in the range 0 to 255.
Integer	Contains integer in the range -32,768 to 32,767.
Currency	-922,337,203,685,477.5808 to 922,337,203,685,477.5807.
Long	Contains integer in the range -2,147,483,648 to 2,147,483,647.

Single   Contains a single-precision, floating-point number in the range -3.402823E38 to -1.401298E-45 for negative values; 1.401298E-45 to 3.402823E38 for positive values.

Double   Contains a double-precision, floating-point number in the range -1.79769313486232E308 to -4.94065645841247E-324 for negative values; 4.94065645841247E-324 to 1.79769313486232E308 for positive values.

Date (Time)   Contains a number that represents a date between January 1, 100 to December 31, 9999.

String   Contains a variable-length string that can be up to approximately 2 billion characters in length.

Object   Contains an object.

Error   Contains an error number.

4.2 Arrays in Vb script

Arrays are used to store the multiple values in contigous locations. We have 2 kinds of arrays in vb script.

1. Fixed-Size array

2. Dynamic Array

Fixed size Array in QTP

Dim A(10) - single dimension
Dim MyTable(5, 10) - multi-dimension

Dynamic Array - size not fixed

Dim MyArray()
ReDim MyArray(25)

We can also create array using Array Function in QTP

A = Array(10,20,30)

B = A(2) ' B is now 30.

4.3 Strings in Vb script

Here is the list of all string functions in QTP.

String functions to extract the part of the string -

left - gets the specified number of characters from the left side of string

mid -gets the specified number of characters from the given position of the string

right - gets the specified number of characters from the right side of string

String functions to remove the spaces from the string -

ltrim - removes the blank spaces from the left side of the string

rtrim - removes the blank spaces from the right side of the string

trim - removes the blank spaces from the left and right side of the string

Other String functions -

String   - Returns a string of the given length with specified character.

Space   - Returns the empty string with given length

strReverse - Reverses the given string

ucase   - Converst the string to upper case

lcase   - Converts the string to lower case

strComp - Compares 2 strings

replace   - replaces the given string str1 from input string say str with other string say str2

len - gets the number of characters in given string

split - splits the string into array using given delimiter

join - forms the string from given array elements

cstr - converts the data type of the variable into String

chr - gets the character corresponding to the given ascii value

Asc - gets the ascii value of the given character.

instr - searches for a substring in a given string and returns the position where the match is found.

InStrRev- searches for a substring in a given string and returns the position where the match is found from the end of the string.

4.4 Date and Time in Vb script

We have below functions to work with date and time.

1. Now – get current timestamp
2. Date – today's date
3. Time – today's time
4. Weekday – gets current weekday
5. Year –gets current year
6. Dateadd – adds date
7. Datediff – finds the difference between 2 dates.

Dateadd function is used to find the future date or old date in QTP.

For example -

Let say you are testing a trading application where you need to calculate the settlement date for a given trade with trade date as say today.

Now the formula for finding the settlement date is -

settlement date = trade date + 3 business days

In such scenarios you will have to add 3 business days to given trade date.

You can make use of dateadd function in QTP.

print dateadd("d",3,now)

Above statement will add 3 days to current date and return the date.

You can also find any previous date using above syntax.

print dateadd("d",-1,now)

This will calculate yesterday's date

print dateadd("d",1,now)

This will calculate tomorrow's date

Syntax of DateAdd function in QTP.

Dateadd(interval_Type, Interval_Units, date)

Interval Type can be of below types.

1. yyyy - Year
2. m - Month
3. d - Day
4. h - Hour
5. n - Minute
6. s - Second

4.5 File System Object

Filesystemobject is used to work with files and folders in vbscript.

Sample script below creates the text file and writes some data in it using filesystemobject.

```
Set fso = CreateObject("Scripting.FileSystemObject")
 Set MyFile = fso.CreateTextFile("d:\mytestfile.txt", True)
 MyFile.WriteLine("This is my  test.")
MyFile.Close
```

Below table shows all methods and properties of the filesystem object.

Object/Collection	Description

FileSystemObject	Main object. Contains methods and properties that allow you to create, delete, gain information about, and generally manipulate drives, folders, and files. Many of the methods associated with this object duplicate those in other FSO objects; they are provided for convenience.
Drive	Object. Contains methods and properties that allow you to gather information about a drive attached to the system, such as its share name and how much room is available. Note that a "drive" isn't necessarily a hard disk, but can be a CD-ROM drive, a RAM disk, and so forth. A drive doesn't need to be physically attached to the system; it can be also be logically connected through a network.
Drives	Collection. Provides a list of the drives attached to the system, either physically or logically. The Drives collection includes all drives, regardless of type. Removable-media drives need not have media inserted for them to appear in this collection.

File	Object. Contains methods and properties that allow you to create, delete, or move a file. Also allows you to query the system for a file name, path, and various other properties.
Files	Collection. Provides a list of all files contained within a folder.
Folder	Object. Contains methods and properties that allow you to create, delete, or move folders. Also allows you to query the system for folder names, paths, and various other properties.
Folders	Collection. Provides a list of all the folders within a Folder.
TextStream	Object. Allows you to read and write text files.

4.6 Dictionary Object

A Dictionary object is the equivalent of a PERL associative array. Items can be any form of data, and are stored in the array. Each item is associated with a unique key. The key is used to retrieve an individual item and is usually an integer or a string, but can be anything except an array.

Dictionary Methods	Add
	Exists
	Items
	Keys
	Remove
	RemoveAll
Dictionary Properties	Count
	Item
	Key

4.7 Regular Expressions

A regular expression is a string that describes or matches a set of strings. It is often called a pattern as it describes set of strings.

Using the Backslash Character

A backslash (\) instructs QuickTest to treat the next character as a literal character, if it is otherwise a special character

For example:

w matches the character w

\w is a special character that matches any word character including underscore

For example, in QTP, while entering the URL of a website,

http://mercurytours.mercuryinteractive.com

The period would be mistaken as an indication of a regular expression. To indicate that the period is not part of a regular expression, you would enter it as follows:

mercurytours\.mercuryinteractive\.com Note: If a backslash character is used before a character that has no special meaning, the backslash is ignored. For example, \z matches z.

Special characters and sequences are used in writing patterns for regular expressions. The following table describes and gives an example of the characters and sequences that can be used.

Character	Description
\	Marks the next character as either a special character or a literal. For example, "n" matches the character "n". "\n" matches a newline character. The sequence "\\" matches "\" and "\(" matches "(".
^	Matches the beginning of input.
$	Matches the end of input.
*	Matches the preceding character zero or more times. For example, "zo*" matches either "z" or "zoo".
+	Matches the preceding character one or more times. For example, "zo+" matches "zoo" but not "z".
?	Matches the preceding character zero or one time. For example, "a?ve?" matches

	the "ve" in "never".
.	Matches any single character except a newline character.
(pattern)	Matches *pattern* and remembers the match. The matched substring can be retrieved from the resulting **Matches** collection, using Item **[0]...[n]**. To match parentheses characters ( ), use "\(" or "\)".
x|y	Matches either *x* or *y*. For example, "z|wood" matches "z" or "wood". "(z|w)oo" matches "zoo" or "wood".
{*n*}	*n* is a nonnegative integer. Matches exactly *n* times. For example, "o{2}" does not match the "o" in "Bob," but matches the first two o's in "foooood".
{*n*,}	*n* is a nonnegative integer. Matches at least *n* times. For example, "o{2,}" does not match the "o" in "Bob" and matches all the o's in "foooood." "o{1,}" is equivalent to "o+". "o{0,}" is equivalent to "o*".
{*n,m*}	*m* and *n* are nonnegative integers. Matches at least *n* and at most *m* times. For example, "o{1,3}" matches the first three o's in "fooooood." "o{0,1}" is equivalent to "o?".

[*xyz*]	A character set. Matches any one of the enclosed characters. For example, "[abc]" matches the "a" in "plain".
[^*xyz*]	A negative character set. Matches any character not enclosed. For example, "[^abc]" matches the "p" in "plain".
[*a-z*]	A range of characters. Matches any character in the specified range. For example, "[a-z]" matches any lowercase alphabetic character in the range "a" through "z".
[^*m-z*]	A negative range characters. Matches any character not in the specified range. For example, "[m-z]" matches any character not in the range "m" through "z".
\b	Matches a word boundary, that is, the position between a word and a space. For example, "er\b" matches the "er" in "never" but not the "er" in "verb".
\B	Matches a non-word boundary. "ea*r\B" matches the "ear" in "never early".
\d	Matches a digit character. Equivalent to [0-9].
\D	Matches a non-digit character. Equivalent to [^0-9].

\f	Matches a form-feed character.
\n	Matches a newline character.
\r	Matches a carriage return character.
\s	Matches any white space including space, tab, form-feed, etc. Equivalent to "[\f\n\r\t\v]".
\S	Matches any nonwhite space character. Equivalent to "[^ \f\n\r\t\v]".
\t	Matches a tab character.
\v	Matches a vertical tab character.
\w	Matches any word character including underscore. Equivalent to "[A-Za-z0-9_]".
\W	Matches any non-word character. Equivalent to "[^A-Za-z0-9_]".
\num	Matches *num*, where *num* is a positive integer. A reference back to remembered matches. For example, "(.)\1" matches two consecutive identical characters.
\n	Matches *n*, where *n* is an octal escape value. Octal escape values must be 1, 2, or 3 digits long. For example, "\11" and "\011" both match a tab character. "\0011" is the equivalent of "\001" & "1". Octal escape values must not exceed

	256. If they do, only the first two digits comprise the expression. Allows ASCII codes to be used in regular expressions.
\x*n*	Matches *n*, where *n* is a hexadecimal escape value. Hexadecimal escape values must be exactly two digits long. For example, "\x41" matches "A". "\x041" is equivalent to "\x04" & "1". Allows ASCII codes to be used in regular expressions.

Function **RegExpTest**(patrn, strng)

```
Set regEx = New RegExp   ' Create a regular expression.
regEx.Pattern = patrn   ' Set pattern.
regEx.IgnoreCase = True   ' Set case insensitivity.
regEx.Global = True   ' Set global applicability.
Set Matches = regEx.Execute(strng)   ' Execute search.
For Each Match in Matches   ' Iterate Matches collection.
   RetStr = RetStr & "Match found at position "
   RetStr = RetStr & Match.FirstIndex & ". Match Value is '"
   RetStr = RetStr & Match.Value & "'." & vbCRLF
```

```
  Next
  RegExpTest = RetStr

End Function


MsgBox(RegExpTest("is.", "IS1 is2 IS3 is4"))


Function ReplaceTest(patrn, replStr)

  Dim regEx, str1          ' Create variables.
  str1 = "The quick brown fox jumped over the lazy dog."
  Set regEx = New RegExp        ' Create regular expression.
  regEx.Pattern = patrn        ' Set pattern.
  regEx.IgnoreCase = True        ' Make case insensitive.
  ReplaceTest = regEx.Replace(str1, replStr)   ' Make replacement.

End Function
```

4.8 Difference between dictionary and array

The Dictionary object is used to store information in name/value pairs (referred to as key and item). The Dictionary object might seem similar to Arrays, however, the Dictionary object is a more desirable solution to manipulate related data.

Keys are used to identify the items in a Dictionary object

You do not have to call ReDim to change the size of the Dictionary object

When deleting an item from a Dictionary, the remaining items will automatically shift up

Dictionaries cannot be multidimensional, Arrays can

Dictionaries have more built-in functions than Arrays

Dictionaries work better than arrays on accessing random elements frequently

Dictionaries work better than arrays on locating items by their content

4.9 Working with outlook

Vbscript can be used to automate Microsoft outlook

Microsoft Outlook Example

```
Set Outlook = CreateObject("Outlook.Application")
Dim Message 'As Outlook.MailItem
Set Message = Outlook.CreateItem(olMailItem)
With Message
.Subject = Subject
.HTMLBody = TextBody
.Recipients.Add (aTo)
Const olOriginator = 0
.Send
End With
End Sub
```

4.10 Working with Excel in vbscript

Microsoft Excel Example

```
Set xl = CreateObject("Excel.Application")
xl.Workbooks.Open "newbook.xls"
Worksheets("Sheet1").Cells(5, 3).Font.Size = 14

set a = createobject("Excel.Application")
set wb = a.workbooks.add()
```

```
a.visible = true
msgbox a.worksheets.count
wb.saveas ("c:\abc.xls")
'set ws = wb.worksheets(0)
'wb.save
a.quit
set a = nothing
```

5. WSH and WMI

5.1 WSH

The illustration that follows represents the Windows Script Host Object Model hierarchy.

Wscript

Wshshell   – *Wshshortcut, Wshurlshortcut, Wshenvironment, Wshspecialfolders, WshscriptExec*

Wshnetwork

Wshcontroller   – *wshremote, wshremoteerror*

Wsharguments – *wshnamed, wshunnamed*

```
WScript
  WshArguments
    WshNamed
    WshUnnamed
  WshController
    WshRemote
      WshRemoteError
  WshNetwork
  WshShell
    WshShortcut
    WshUrlShortCut
    WshEnvironment
    WshSpecialFolders
    WshScriptExec
```

The Windows Script Host object model provides a logical, systematic way to perform many administrative tasks. The set of COM interfaces it provides can be placed into two main categories:

The following table is a list of the WSH objects and the typical tasks associated with them.

Object	What you can do with this object
WScript Object	Set and retrieve command line arguments
	Determine the name of the script file
	Determine the host file name (wscript.exe or cscript.exe)
	Determine the host version information
	Create, connect to, and disconnect from COM objects
	Sink events
	Stop a script's execution programmatically
	Output information to the default output device (for example, a dialog

	box or the command line)
	Arguments | FullName | Interactive | Name | Path | ScriptFullName
	| ScriptName | StdErr | StdIn | StdOut | Version
	Methods
	CreateObject | ConnectObject | DisconnectObject | Echo
	| GetObject |Quit | Sleep
WshArguments Object	Access the entire set of command-line arguments
WshNamed Object	Access the set of named command-line arguments
WshUnnamed Object	Access the set of unnamed command-line arguments
WshNetwork Object	Connect to and disconnect from network shares and network printers

	Map and unmap network shares
	Access information about the currently logged-on user
	ComputerName Property | UserDomain Property | UserName Property
	AddWindowsPrinterConnection Method | AddPrinterConnection Method | EnumNetworkDrives Method | EnumPrinterConnection Method | MapNetworkDrive Method | RemoveNetworkDrive Method | RemovePrinterConnection Method | SetDefaultPrinter Method
WshController Object	Create a remote script process using the Controller method **CreateScript**() Dim Controller, RemoteScript Set Controller = WScript.CreateObject("WSHController") Set RemoteScript = Controller.**CreateScript**("test.js", "remoteserver") WScript.ConnectObject RemoteScript, "remote_"

	RemoteScript.Execute Do While RemoteScript.Status <> 2 　WScript.Sleep 100 Loop WScript.DisconnectObject RemoteScript
WshRemote Object	Remotely administer computer systems on a computer network Programmatically manipulate other programs/scripts
WshRemoteError Object	Access the error information available when a remote script (a WshRemote object) terminates as a result of a script error
WshShell Object	Run a program locally Manipulate the contents of the registry

	Create a shortcut
	Access a system folder
	Manipulate environment variables (such as WINDIR, PATH, or PROMPT)
	CurrentDirectory Property | Environment Property | SpecialFolders Property
	Methods
	AppActivate Method | CreateShortcut Method | ExpandEnvironmentStrings Method | LogEvent Method | Popup Method | RegDelete Method | RegRead Method | RegWrite Method | Run Method | SendKeys Method | Exec Method
WshShortcut Object	Programmatically create a shortcut
WshSpecialFolders Object	Access any of the Windows Special Folders
WshUrlShortcut Object	Programmatically create a shortcut to an Internet resource

WshEnvironment Object	Access any of the environment variables (such as WINDIR, PATH, or PROMPT)
	Set WshShell= WScript.CreateObject("WScript.Shell")
	Set WshSysEnv = WshShell.Environment("SYSTEM")
	WScript.Echo WshSysEnv("NUMBER_OF_PROCESSORS")
WshScriptExec Object	Determine status and error information about a script run with Exec()
	Access the StdIn, StdOut, and StdErr

5.2 WMI

WMI allows scripting languages like VBScript or Windows PowerShell to manage Microsoft Windows personal computers and servers, both locally and remotely

Below example illustrates how we can use WMI to get the information about the running processes in the system.

```
On Error Resume Next
StrComputer = "."
Set objWMIService = GetObject ("winmgmts:\\" & strComputer &
"\root\cimv2")
Set colItems = objWMIService.ExecQuery ("Select * from
Win32_Process",, 48)

For Each objItem in colItems
    Wscript.Echo "Caption: " & objItem.Caption
    Wscript.Echo "CreationClassName: " & objItem.CreationClassName
    Wscript.Echo "CreationDate: " & objItem.CreationDate
    Wscript.Echo "CSCreationClassName: " &
objItem.CSCreationClassName
Next
```